To the girls of Malvern St James Preparator – P.G.

The publishers would like to thank the following for permission to include copyright material reproduced in this book.

'Unfolding Bud' copyright © Naoshi Koriyama 1987, from *Rhythm and Rhyme*, ed. Elaine Hamilton, OUP Australia, 1987; 'Argumentative' copyright © Carol Ann Duffy 2003, from 'Seven Deadly Adjectives' in *The Good Child's Guide to Rock and Roll*, Faber and Faber, 2003; 'To Pass the Time' copyright © Richard Edwards 1987, from *Island of the Children*, ed. Angela Huth, Orchard Books, 1987; 'Little Girl, Be Careful What You Say' copyright © Carl Sandburg 1969, 1970 Lilian Steichen Sandberg, Trustee, from *The Complete Poems of Carl Sandburg*, Revised and Expanded Edition, by permission of Houghton Mifflin Harcourt Publishing Company; 'An Owl Flew into My Bedroom Once' copyright © Jan Dean 1999, *from Read Me 2*, ed. Gaby Morgan, Macmillan Children's Books, 1999, by permission of the author; 'A Hatchling's Song' copyright © Judy Sierra 1998, from *Antarctic Antics: A Book of Penguin Poems*, by permission of Harcourt Inc; 'My Sari' copyright © Debjani Chatterjee 1998, from *Unzip Your Lips*, ed. Paul Cookson, Macmillan Children's Books, 1998, by permission of the author; 'Huff' copyright © Wendy Cope 2000, from *I'm in a Mood Today*, ed. John Foster, OUP, 2000, by permission of United Agents on behalf of the author; 'An Enquiring Mind' copyright © Douglas Houston 1996, from *Casting a Spell*, ed. Angela Huth, Orchard Books, 1996; 'Joy at the Sound' copyright © Roger McGough 2002, from *Good Enough to Eat*, Puffin, 2002, by permission of United Agents on behalf of the author; 'Stepmother' copyright ©Jean Kenward 1993, from *All in the Family*, ed. John Foster, OUP, 1993; 'The Moon Speaks' copyright © James Carter 2009, from *Greetings, Earthlings!, Space Poems*, Macmillan Children's Books, 2009, by permission of the author; 'Isn't My Name Magical?' copyright © James Berry 1999, from *Isn't My Name Magical?*, Longman, 1999, by permission of Peters, Fraser and Dunlop; 'Ode to my Oldest Best Shoes' copyright © Kwame Dawes 2002, from *Hello New!*, ed. John Agard, Orchard Books, 2002; 'Celebration' copyright © Ann Ziety 1995, from *Bumwigs and Earbeetles*, ed. Wendy Metcalf, Bodley Head, 1995; 'in Just' copyright © 1991 the Trustees for the E.E. Cummings Trust and George James Firmage, from *The Complete Poems of E.E. Cummings 1904-1962*, ed. George J Firmage, by permission of W.W. Norton and Co; 'At Night' copyright © Raymond McCormack 1966, from *Once Around the Sun*, ed. Brian Thompson, OUP, 1966; 'I'm in a Rotten Mood' copyright © Jack Prelutsky 1986, from *The New Kid on the Block*, Harper Collins, 1986; 'Grandad' copyright © Kit Wright 1978, from *Rabbiting On and Other Poems*, Young Lions, 1978, by permission of the author; 'My Dad is Very Keen on Sport' copyright © Trevor Harvey, from *Fun with Poems*, ed. Irene Yates, Brilliant Publications, 2000, by permission of the author; 'Sun is Laughing' copyright © Grace Nichols 1994, from *A Caribbean Dozen*, Walker Books, 1994, by permission of Curtis Brown Ltd; 'GHEAUGHTEIGHPTOUGH spells POTATO' copyright © Michael Rosen, from *Walking the Bridge of Your Nose*, Kingfisher, by permission of the author; 'Ice' copyright © Jim Wong-Chu 1986, from *Chinatown Ghosts*, Arsenal Press, 1986; 'The Emperor's Cat' copyright © Lemn Sissay 2000, from *The Emperor's Watchmaker*, Bloomsbury, 2000, by permission of David Higham Associates on behalf of the author; 'Little Sister' copyright © Benjamin Zephaniah 1995, from *Talking Turkeys*, Puffin, 1995, by permission of United Artists on behalf of the author; 'Who is de Girl?' copyright © John Agard 1997, from *Get Back Pimple*, Puffin, 1997, by permission of Caroline Sheldon Literary Agency on behalf of the author.

The publishers apologise to any copyright holders they were unable to trace and would be pleased to hear from them.

JANETTA OTTER-BARRY BOOKS

A is Amazing copyright © Frances Lincoln Limited 2012
This selection copyright © Wendy Cooling 2012
Illustrations copyright © Piet Grobler 2012

First published in Great Britain in 2012 by
Frances Lincoln Children's Books, 4 Torriano Mews,
Torriano Avenue, London NW5 2RZ
www.franceslincoln.com

A catalogue record for this book is available from the British Library.

ISBN 978-1-84780-255-2

Illustrated with pencil and watercolours

Set in Bliss

Printed in China by C&C Offset Printing Co., Ltd in May 2012

1 3 5 7 9 8 6 4 2

AMAZING

Unfolding Bud

One is amazed
By a water-lily bud
Unfolding
With each passing day,
Taking on a richer colour
And new dimensions.

One is not amazed,
At a first glance,
By a poem,
Which is as tight-closed
As a tiny bud.

Yet one is surprised
To see the poem
Gradually unfolding,
Revealing its rich inner self,
As one reads it
Again
And over again.

Naoshi Koriyama
Japan

8

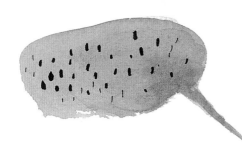

ARGUMENTATIVE

Argumentative
(from Seven Deadly Adjectives)

She'd argue black was white
to be right, that blue was red
to say the last word to be said,
that yellow was green, a king
was really a queen, that bright day
was night.

　　　　　She'd have it that
the long was the short of it,
the bottom line was only the tip
of the iceberg and fire was ice, insist
that the hill of a mole in the grass
was a mountain, the spill from a hole

in a glass was a fountain. She'd say
home was away, in out, truth doubt,
reason was madness, goodness badness,
argue the toss till heads were tails, peanuts
were huge rocks, small fry were giant whales
in the churning, quarrelling sea.

Carol Ann Duffy
UK

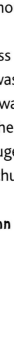

BORED

To Pass the Time

When I'm bored I count things:
Cornflakes, cars,
Pencils, people, leaves on trees,
Raindrops, stars,
Footsteps, heartbeats, pebbles, waves,
Gaggles, herds and flocks,
Freckles, blinks per minute,
The ticks
Of clocks.
Eighty-seven lamp-posts
Line our street.
Did you know a wood-louse has
Fourteen feet?
And – two vests, four pairs of pants, six shirts, two
T-shirts, one pair of jeans, two other pairs of trousers,
one pair of shorts, three belts, three pullovers, one of
them without sleeves, a raincoat, a jacket, two pairs of
pyjamas, one glove, one tie and eleven socks are
The clothes I've got
In five drawers and one wardrobe:
I'm bored
A lot.

Richard Edwards
UK

10

Little Girl, Be Careful What You Say

Little girl, be careful what you say
when you make talk with words, words –
for words are made of syllables
and syllables, child, are made of air –
and air is so thin – air is the breath of God –
air is finer than fire or mist,
finer than water or moonlight,
finer than spiderwebs in the moon,
finer than water-flowers in the morning:
   and words are strong, too,
   stronger than rocks or steel,
stronger than potatoes, corn, fish, cattle,
and soft, too, soft as little pigeon-eggs,
soft as the music of hummingbird wings.
   So, little girl, when you speak greetings,
when you tell jokes, make wishes or prayers,
   be careful, be careless, be careful.
   Be what you wish to be.

Carl Sandburg
USA

11

DREAMY

An Owl Flew in my Bedroom Once

My attic bedroom had two windows –
One that opened high above the street
And a skylight – a tile of thick glass
Like a see-through slate.
And through it fell the moonlight
Coring the darkness like an apple-peeler.
Suddenly in that long cylinder of light
Appeared the owl, mysterious and grey
In that cold moon.
He flew in silently – a piece of night adrift –
Escaped. He circled, didn't settle
On the banister or rail.
There was no rattle of his talons,
No gripe or stomp
To make him solid with their sound,
He simply floated in – turned wide – and floated out...
In the morning there was nothing
No down or limy dropping
Nothing to prove he'd ever been at all.

An owl flew in my bedroom once, I think.

Jan Dean
UK

A Hatchling's Song

I'm almost hatched!
I'm almost hatched!
I'm small, I'm wet,
I'm not out yet.

I'm pecking hard,
I'm pecking hard.
I'm tired, I'm weak,
It hurts my beak.

My head's outside,
My head's outside.
The moon is bright –
The world's so white!

I'm really hatched,
I'm really hatched.
At last I'm free.
Hey, Dad, it's me!
I'm really hatched.

Judy Sierra
USA

FRIENDLY

Oath of Friendship

Shang ya!
I want to be your friend
For ever and ever without break or decay.
When the hills are all flat
And the rivers are all dry,
When it lightens and thunders in winter,
When it rains and snows in summer,
When Heaven and Earth mingle –
Not till then will I part from you.

Anon
(China)

GOOD

My Sari

Saris hang on the washing line:
a rainbow in our neighbourhood.
This little orange one is mine,
it has a mango leaf design.
I wear it as a Rani would.
It wraps around me like sunshine,
it ripples silky down my spine,
and I stand tall and feel so good.

Debjani Chatterjee
India/UK

14

Huff

I am in a tremendous huff –
Really, really bad.
It isn't any ordinary huff –
It's one of the best I've had.

I plan to keep it up for a month
Or maybe for a year
And you needn't think you can make me smile
Or talk to you. No fear.

I can do without you and her and them –
Too late to make amends.
I'll think deep thoughts on my own for a while,
Then find some better friends.

And they'll be wise enough to see
That they should behave with proper respect
Towards somebody like me.

I do like being in a huff –
Cold fury is so heady.
I've been like this for half an hour
And it's cheered me up already.

Perhaps I'll give them another chance,
Now I'm feeling stronger,
But they'd better watch out – my next big huff
Could last much, much, much longer.

Wendy Cope
UK

15

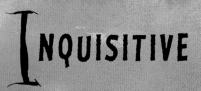 INQUISITIVE

An Enquiring Mind

– for Iggy

Dad, who invented numbers
And how did they agree
The order they should go in,
How many there should be?

Why is it lead's so heavy
While balsa wood's so light?
If ghosts aren't real, why was I scared
Of ghosts the other night?

You told me how the moon pulls tides,
Why stars fade when night's done
(Seems obvious now: they go quite pale
Competing with the sun).

I asked you what the clouds were,
So now I think I know
That sky-fluff's water-vapour
Borne where the winds will blow;

You said that stuff called chlorophyll
Makes leaves and grasses green –
But why are roses mainly red
And a blue one's never seen?

Why is it mountains are so big
And why do roofs have tiles?
Is it further to America
In kilometres or miles?

For some time I've been wondering
How apple cores go brown,
And why are colours what they are?
Can water-snakes still drown?

Thanks for the encyclopaedia, Dad.
The dictionary's good, too;
But when it comes to finding out
It's quicker asking you.

Douglas Houston
UK

Joy at the Sound

Joy at the silver birch in the morning sunshine
Joy at the spring-green of its fingertips

Joy at the swirl of cold milk in the blue bowl
Joy at the blink of its bubbles

Joy at the cat revving up on the lawn
Joy at the frogs that leapfrog to freedom

Joy at the screen as it fizzes to life
Joy at The Simpsons, Lisa and Bart

Joy at the dentist: 'Fine, see you next year!'
Joy at the school gates: 'Closed'.

Joy at the silver withholding the chocolate
Joy at the poem, two verses to go

Joy at the zing of the strings of the racquet
Joy at the bounce of the bright yellow ball

Joy at the key unlocking the door
Joy at the sound of her voice in the hall

Roger McGough
UK

KIND

Stepmother

My stepmother
is really nice.
She ought to wear
a label.
I don't come in
with a latch key, now –
my tea is on
the table.
She doesn't nag at me
or shout.
I often hear her
singing.
I'm glad my dad
had wedding bells –
and I hope
they go on ringing.

Stepmothers
in fairy tales
are hard and cold
as iron.
There isn't a lie
they wouldn't tell,
or a trick
they wouldn't try on.
But MY stepmother's
warm and true;
she's kind, and cool,
and clever –
Yes! I've a *wicked*
stepmother –
and I hope she stays
for ever!

Jean Kenward
UK

19

Loving

My Love for You

I know you little, I know you lots;
My love for you would fill ten pots,
Fifteen buckets, sixteen cans,
Three teacups and four dishpans.

Traditional

The Moon Speaks

I, the moon,
would like it known – I
never follow people home. I
simply do not have the time. And
neither do I ever shine. For what you
often see at night is me reflecting solar
light. And I'm not cheese! No, none of
these: no mozzarellas, cheddars, bries, all
you'll find here if you please – are my
dusty, empty seas. And cows do not
jump over me. Now that is simply
lunacy! You used to come and
visit me. Oh, do return,
I'm lonely, see.

James Carter
UK

Isn't My Name Magical?

Nobody can see my name on me.
My name is inside
and all over me, unseen
like other people also keep it.
   Isn't my name magic?

My name is mine only.
It tells I am individual,
the only special person it shakes
when I'm wanted.

If I'm with hundreds of people
and my name gets called,
my sound switches me on to answer
like it was my human electricity.
   Isn't that magical?

My name echoes across the playground,
it comes, it demands my attention.
I have to find out who calls,
who wants me for what.
My name gets blurted out in class,
it is a terror, at a bad time,
because somebody is cross.

My name gets called in a whisper
I am happy, because
my name may have touched me
with a loving voice.
    Isn't it all magic?

James Berry
Jamaica/UK

23

NAUGHTY

A Song About Myself

There was a naughty boy
  And a naughty boy was he
He ran away to Scotland
  The people for to see –
      There he found
      That the ground
      Was as hard
      That a yard
      Was as long,
      That a song
      Was as merry,
      That a cherry
      Was as red –
      That lead
      Was as weighty
      That fourscore
      Was as eighty
      That a door
      Was as wooden
      As in England –
      So he stood in
      His shoes
      And he wonder'd
      He stood in his
      Shoes and he wonder'd.

John Keats
UK

Ode to My Oldest Best Shoes

Soft and just the right shape too,
my feet slip in, my toes are giggling,
they know how to make a ball swerve
they get green with grass
and brown with mud
and black with soot
and wet with rain
and smelly and grey
and still feel as right as can be.

There is no sweating or straining
no moaning and groaning
to get my feet to slip right in
it's as if I am floating
or dancing a jig
barefoot in cotton
through nettles and thorns
through garbage heaps
over nails and grass
and still feel as right as can be.

That's why I am crying like a baby
and limping like a jalopy truck
that is why my toes are whining
that they can't breathe or laugh at all
no dirt, no dust
no stones in the toes
no paint and grease
no games in the bush
I'll never feel right again, Mum,
not with these awful new shoes, Mum,
not with these awful new shoes!

Kwame Dawes
Africa/Jamaica

25

ORIGINAL

Celebration

is daring
to be
who we are
it's like dancing
on table tops
while the world spins
and the fear stops
and the waves crash
and the stars glow
and the heart beats
and inside your head
you hear this song
rising
up
like laughter
rising
up
like laughter
rising
up
like a firework
soaring and weightless
to fill the whole sky
with joy

Ann Ziety
UK

in Just-

PUDDLE-WONDERFUL

in Just-
spring   when the world is mud-
luscious the little
lame balloonman

whistles   far   and wee

and eddieandbill come
running from marbles and
piracies and it's
spring

when the world is puddle-wonderful

the queer
old balloonman whistles
far   and   wee
and bettyandisbel come dancing

from hop-scotch and jump-rope and

it's
spring
and
          the

                    goat-footed

balloonMan   whistles
far
and
wee

E.E. Cummings
USA

27

Quiet

At Night

When the tide comes in
and the moon
comes out,
the sea goes to bed
and all is still
as still as can be.

Even the fish
sense the still
and quietly slither
in between the rocks
and seek a place
for night.

The whole world of sea
seems to rest at night.
Even the little waves
creep silently upon
the shore.

Raymond McCormack
Australia

I'm in a Rotten Mood

I'm in a rotten mood today,
a really rotten mood today,
I'm feeling cross,
I'm feeling mean,
I'm jumpy as a jumping bean,
I have an awful attitude –
I'M IN A ROTTEN MOOD!

I'm in a rotten mood today,
a really rotten mood today,
I'm in a snit,
I'm in a stew,
there's nothing that I care to do
but sit all by myself and brood –
I'M IN A ROTTEN MOOD!

I'm in a rotten mood today,
a really rotten mood today,
you'd better stay away from me,
I'm just a lump of misery,
I'm feeling absolutely rude –
I'M IN A ROTTEN MOOD!

Jack Prelutsky
USA

Sad

Grandad

Grandad's dead
And I'm sorry about that.

He'd have a huge black overcoat.
He felt proud in it.
You could have hidden
A football crowd in it.
Far too big –
It was a lousy fit
But Grandad didn't
Mind a bit.
He wore it all winter
With a squashed black hat.

Now he's dead
And I'm sorry about that.

He'd got twelve stories.
I'd heard every one of them
Hundreds of times
But that was the fun of them:
You knew what was coming
So you could join in.
He'd got big hands
And brown, grooved skin
And when he laughed
It knocked you flat.

Now he's dead
And I'm sorry about that.

Kit Wright
UK

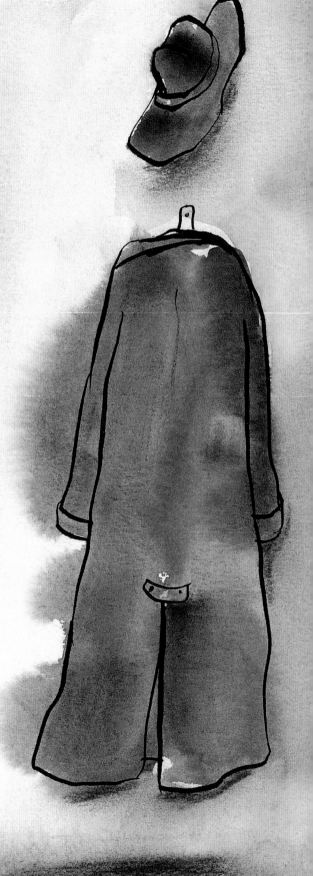

The Secret

We have a secret, just we three,
The robin, and I, and the sweet cherry-tree;
The bird told the tree, and the tree told me,
And nobody knows it but just us three.

But of course the robin knows it best,
Because he built the – I shan't tell the rest;
And laid the four little – something in it –
I'm afraid I shall tell it every minute.

But if the tree and the robin don't peep,
I'll try my best the secret to keep;
Though I know when the little birds fly about
Then the whole secret will be out.

Emily Dickinson
USA

TIRED

My Dad Is Very Keen on Sport

My Dad may be OLD
But he's still keen on sport –
WATCHING IT is bliss!
He's had installed cable TV
To make sure he does not miss
A single
football match goal
  cricketer's bowl
    downhill ski
      golf match tee
        runner's sprint
          ice-skate glint
         judo throw
          rower's row
           rider's jump
            stockcar's bump
            swimmer's stroke
          engine's choke
            basketball score
             or rugby crowd's roar!

BUT after five minutes
He falls asleep
In his armchair

My Dad is living proof that
Although sport may be INSPIRING
It's also VERY tiring...!

Trevor Harvey
UK

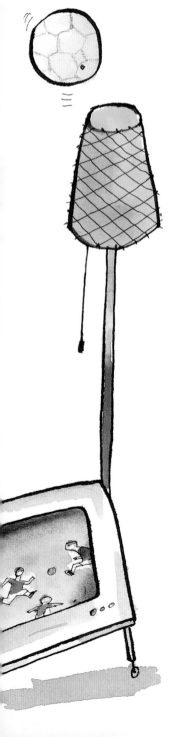

32

Unpredictable

Sun Is Laughing

This morning she got up
on the happy side of bed,
pulled back
the grey sky-curtains
and she poked her head
through the blue window
of heaven,
her yellow laughter
spilling over,
falling broad across the grass,
brightening the washing on the line,
giving more shine
to the back of a ladybug
and buttering up all the world.

Then, without any warning,
as if she was suddenly bored,
or just got sulky
because she could hear no one
giving praise
to her shining ways,
Sun slammed the sky-window close,
plunging the whole world
into greyness once more.
O sun, moody one,
how can we live
without the holiday of your face?

Grace Nichols
Guyana/UK

33

VERY STRANGE

GHEAUGHTEIGHPTOUGH Spells POTATO

How?
GH is P, as in hiccough;
EAU is O, as in beau;
GHT is T, as in naught;
EIGH is A, as in neigh;
PT is T, as in pterodactyl;
OUGH is O, as in though.

Michael Rosen
UK

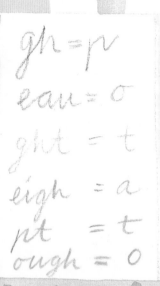

gh = p
eau = o
ght = t
eigh = a
pt = t
ough = o

I Said My Pyjamas

I said my pyjamas,
I slipped on my prayers.
I went up my slippers,
I took off the stairs.
I turned off the bed,
I jumped in the light.
The reason for this...
You gave me a fright!

Anonymous

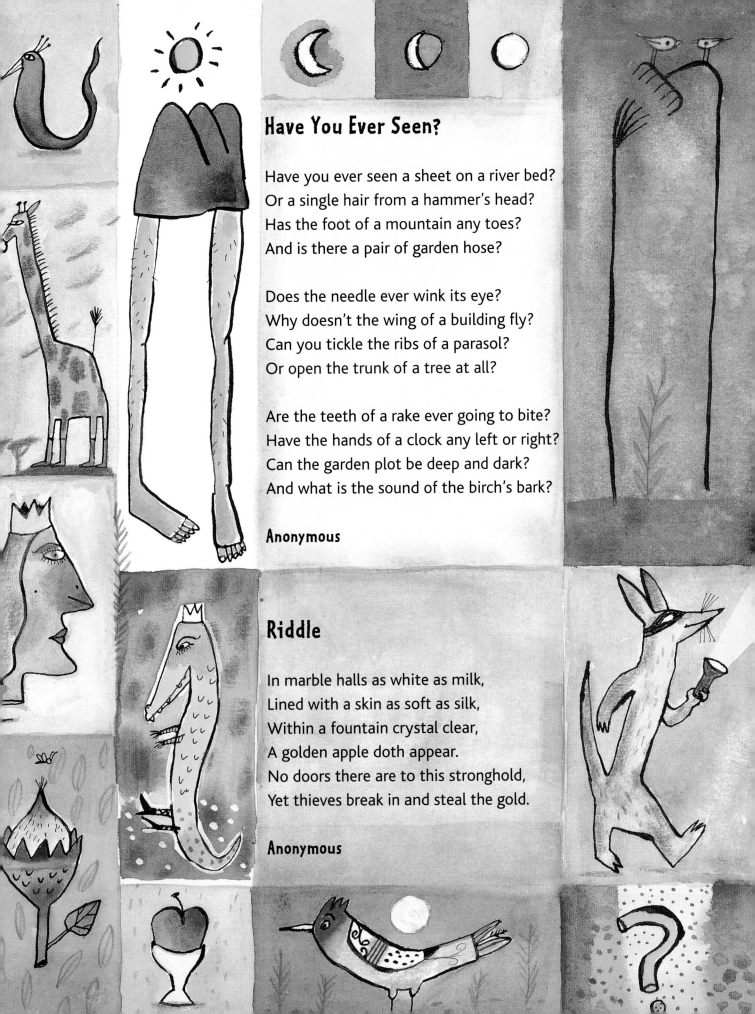

Have You Ever Seen?

Have you ever seen a sheet on a river bed?
Or a single hair from a hammer's head?
Has the foot of a mountain any toes?
And is there a pair of garden hose?

Does the needle ever wink its eye?
Why doesn't the wing of a building fly?
Can you tickle the ribs of a parasol?
Or open the trunk of a tree at all?

Are the teeth of a rake ever going to bite?
Have the hands of a clock any left or right?
Can the garden plot be deep and dark?
And what is the sound of the birch's bark?

Anonymous

Riddle

In marble halls as white as milk,
Lined with a skin as soft as silk,
Within a fountain crystal clear,
A golden apple doth appear.
No doors there are to this stronghold,
Yet thieves break in and steal the gold.

Anonymous

WONDER

Ice

Was the first time
Anyone remembers it happening

The fields froze
In our village
In South China

We broke some
Not knowing what it was
And took it to the junk peddler

He thought it was glass
And traded us a penny for it

He wrapped it up
In an old cloth and placed it
On top of his basket

Of course
The noon day sun melted it

By the time
We came back with more
He had gotten wise

Jim Wong-Chu
China/Canada

Escape at Bedtime

The lights from the parlour and kitchen shone out
Through the blinds and the windows and bars;
And high overhead and all moving about,
There were thousands of millions of stars.
There ne'er were such thousands of leaves on a tree,
Nor of people in church or the Park,
As the crowds of the stars that looked down upon me,
And that glittered and winked in the dark.

The Dog, and the Plough, and the Hunter, and all,
And the star of the sailor, and Mars,
These shone in the sky, and the pail by the wall
Would be half full of water and stars.
They saw me at last, and they chased me with cries,
And they soon had me packed into bed;
But the glory kept shining and bright in my eyes,
And the stars going round in my head.

Robert Louis Stevenson
UK

eXtraordinary

The Emperor's Cat

I'm a sonic superstylish
Cool kind of cat
I wear my own fur coat
And matching fur hat

I got a white Nike streak
All the way down my back
And I got milk from the palace
On tap! You got that

I'm no stray-cat, alley cat
No rat-catching, scally cat
I'm no back-scratching, dilly-dally cat
I'm the cat – you got that

I like the fine things
I eat caviar, only sleep on silk
Only use chauffeur-driven cars
I only drink premium milk

When I need exercise
I send the butler out for a job
Lulu may be a nice canine
But this cat is the top dog

You get what I'm saying here
The emperor is nice, so's his wife,
But he can't catch a mouse
To save his life

They be screaming and hollering
Stood on the table top
And they don't call the butler
Nor that crazy lazy dog

I walk into their room
On hearing all this fuss
I stare that mouse in the eye
'This palace ain't big enough for two of us'

I use my hip hypnosis
Get that mouse in a daze
I say 'You are feeling sleepy
So get outa my paLACE (ahem)'

And off it goes, just like that
Cause I am a class act
I'm hypnotic and supersonic
I'm THE cat – you got that.

Fact. I'm the prime minister
Of cats a class act, got that fact
I'm Action packed. Government backed
I'm THE cat – you got that.

Lemn Sissay
Africa/UK

Little Sister

That's my little sister
Just five minutes old
Already seeking something
To bite and chew and hold,
That's my little sister
Already going bald
I can't just call her sister
So what will she be called?

I want to call her Carol
But all carols are hymns
I want to call her Jimmy
But I always visit gyms,
I want to call her Spotty
But she may punch my nose
I will not call her Rosy
She don't look like a rose.

When I hear her crying
I want to call her *loud*
If she's the type for talking
I may call her a *crowd*,
If she's good at singing
I'll call her *nightingale*
If she keeps on grinning
She'll make the doctors wail.

The doctors called her beauty
But Beauty is a horse
The nurses called her cutey
Being polite of course,
My Mummy and my Daddy
Just don't have an idea
We don't have a name ready
But we're so glad she's here.

Benjamin Zephaniah
UK

41

ZESTFUL

Who Is de Girl?

Who is de girl dat kick de ball
then jump for it over de wall

sallyann is a girl so full-o zest
sallyann is a girl dat just can't rest

who is de girl dat pull de hair
of de bully and make him scare

sallyann is a girl so full-o zest
sallyann is a girl dat just can't rest

who is de girl who bruise she knee
when she fall from de mango tree

sallyann is a girl so full-o zest
sallyann is a girl dat just can't rest

who is de girl who set de pace
when boys and girls dem start to race

sallyann is a girl so full-o zest
sallyann is a girl dat just can't rest

John Agard
Guyana/UK

42

FIZZY

Lizzie

Lizzie, Lizzie, spinning top,
Ever dancing, never stop.
Dancing in the morning dew,
Barefoot tap, one two, one two.

Lizzie, Lizzie, spinning top,
Ever dancing never stop.
Dancing in the sun's warm rays,
Shining brightly at midday.

Lizzie, Lizzie, spinning top,
Ever dancing, never stop.
Dancing as the sun sinks low,
Setting all the lake aglow.

Now she's lying in her bed,
Rosy pillow 'neath her head.
Round the fence a dream comes creeping,
Softly now... for Lizzie's sleeping.

Traditional
Poland

About the poets

John Agard, who grew up in Guyana, is popular throughout Britain as a playwright, poet and performer. He has won many awards for his perceptive, humorous writing.

James Berry was born and grew up in Jamaica but has lived in England for many years. He is a distinguished prize-winning writer of poetry and short stories.

James Carter ia a prize-winning poet, guitarist and educational writer. He travels widely, giving brilliant performances and workshops. He lives in England with his wife, two daughters, three cats and four guitars.

Debjani Chatterjee is an Indian-born poet who lives in Sheffield, England. Her work is popular in anthologies for children. After many years teaching and lecturing, she is now a full-time writer who has written and edited over 50 books.

Wendy Cope is a much-loved British poet, known for her wit and humour and for her ability to parody others, especially contemporary writers. She writes for adults but many of her poems have great child-appeal.

E.E. Cummings, the American poet, lived from 1894-1962 and was one of the most popular voices of the twentieth century. His poetry is noted for its innovative typography and lack of punctuation, and has often given children the freedom to write their own very original poems.

Kwame Dawes was born in Ghana in 1962 but spent most of his childhood in Jamaica where he was greatly influenced by the rhythms and textures of the island. He is Poet-in-Residence at the University of South Carolina and director of the Calabash Literary Festival in Jamaica.

Jan Dean is a British poet and novelist whose poems have appeared in over 100 anthologies. She works as a writer-in-schools and has performed at the major literary festivals.

Emily Dickinson (1830-1886) lived a reclusive life in New England, USA. She is acknowledged as one of the most original poets of the English-speaking world. Her poems, seemingly simple, contain layers of meaning and provoke much thought.

Carol Ann Duffy was appointed Poet Laureate in 2009, the first female poet to be so honoured. She writes poetry for adults and children and has won many awards in the UK, where she is one of the most read and best-loved poets.

Richard Edwards is a British poet who lives in Scotland. He is a master of light verse and his bright, rich and warm poems appeal to children and parents. His poetry appears in many anthologies as well as in his own acclaimed collections.

Trevor Harvey was born in London and, now retired from his post as a university lecturer, he writes very popular comic poetry for children.

Douglas Houston was born in Cardiff, Wales, in 1947. He is a writer, poet and academic and his poetry has been published in many anthologies.

John Keats was born in London in 1795 and died in Rome in 1821. In his short life he produced some extraordinary poetry that has stood the test of time. His life and his poems continue to fascinate all lovers of language.

Jean Kenward was born in 1920 and is known worldwide for her poems for children, which have appeared in numerous anthologies and been heard regularly on radio. She lives in Hertfordshire, England.

Naoshi Koriyama was born on one of the Amami Islands of Southern Japan in 1926 and is now a professor of literature at Tokyo University. He is a poet and enjoys translating Japanese poems into English.

Raymond McCormack lives in Australia.

Roger McGough is one of Britain's most popular poets and is a brilliant performer. His poems, for children and adults, are a great blend of wit and compassion. He travels the world reading his poetry.

Grace Nichols spent her early years in Guyana in a home filled with storytelling. She now lives in the UK where she is very well-known and writes poetry for adults and children.

Jack Prelutsky lives in Seattle, USA, and has been writing inventive and often funny poetry for children for over 30 years. In 2006 he became the first ever American Children's Poet Laureate.

Michael Rosen is a bestselling and hugely influential poet, performer and broadcaster, who was the Children's Laureate from 2007-2009. He lives in London.

Carl Sandburg, the highly respected American poet, lived from 1878-1967. His writing was wide-ranging and often political and he was given a Pulitzer Prize in 1940 for his biography of Abraham Lincoln.

Judy Sierra was born in Washington DC and now lives in Oregon. She worked as a children's librarian, in children's television and as an entertainer before becoming a full-time writer.

Lemn Sissay is an award-winning British writer and broadcaster of Ethiopian and Eritrean parents. He became Artist-in-Residence at London's Southbank Centre in 2008 and is seen regularly on TV.

Robert Louis Stevenson was born in Edinburgh, Scotland, in 1850 and died in Samoa in 1894. He is best remembered for the novel *Treasure Island* and his collection of poetry, *A Child's Garden of Verses*.

Jim Wong-Chu lives in Vancouver, Canada where he was the founder of the Asian Canadian Writers Workshop. He is a well-known poet and anthologist.

Kit Wright won a scholarship to Oxford University and worked as a lecturer in Canada before becoming a full-time writer. He has published over 25 books of poetry for children and adults and is the winner of many literary awards.

Benjamin Zephaniah is a celebrated performance poet with a finger firmly on the pulse of today's Britain. As well as poetry collections, he has published acclaimed novels for children.

Ann Ziety is a British poet and anthologist, and the editor of *Bumwigs and Earbeetles and other Unspeakable Delights*.